Exploring Robotics

Competition Robots

Lisa Idzikowski

Lerner Publications ◆ Minneapolis

For my family

Lerner Publications Company
An imprint of Lerner Publishing Group, Inc.
241 First Avenue North
Minneapolis, MN 55401 USA

For reading levels and more information, look up this title at www.lernerbooks.com.

Main body text set in Adrianna Regular.
Typeface provided by Chank.

Editor: Brianna Kaiser

Library of Congress Cataloging-in-Publication Data

Names: Idzikowski, Lisa, author.
Title: Competition robots / Lisa Idzikowski.
Description: Minneapolis : Lerner Publications, [2024] | Series: Searchlight books. Exploring robotics | Includes bibliographical references and index. | Audience: Ages 8–11 | Audience: Grades 4–6 | Summary: "Competition robots are created by young people. Explore the kinds of robots that have been used in competitions, the people who make them, and the past, present, and future of competition robots"— Provided by publisher.
Identifiers: LCCN 2022038348 (print) | LCCN 2022038349 (ebook) | ISBN 9781728476766 (library binding) | ISBN 9798765603659 (paperback) | ISBN 9798765600030 (ebook)
Subjects: LCSH: Robotics—Competitions—Juvenile literature. | Robots—Juvenile literature.
Classification: LCC TJ211.2 .I39 2024 (print) | LCC TJ211.2 (ebook) | DDC 629.8/92079—dc23/eng/20220919

LC record available at https://lccn.loc.gov/2022038348
LC ebook record available at https://lccn.loc.gov/2022038349

Manufactured in the United States of America
1-52257-50697-11/11/2022

Table of Contents

Chapter 1

GETTING COMPETITIVE . . . 4

Chapter 2

EARLY ROBOT COMPETITIONS . . . 10

Chapter 3

MANY CHALLENGES . . . 14

Chapter 4

FUTURE ROBOTICS . . . 23

Glossary • 30
Learn More • 31
Index • 32

GETTING COMPETITIVE

In 2022, the National Aeronautics and Space Administration (NASA) hosted the Lunabotics Junior Contest. The contest challenged students from kindergarten through twelfth grade to create a robot that could be used in future missions on the moon. The robot had to be able to dig up soil from one area of the lunar south pole and move it to a future Artemis moon base about 328 feet (100 m) away. Robots could be no larger than 3.5 x 2 x 2 feet (1.1 x 0.6 x 0.6 m).

Over two thousand students sent drawings, photos, and diagrams to NASA. Then about five hundred judges voted on the best model robots. Nine-year-old Lucia Grisanti won the younger-grade competition. Her solar-powered robot, Olympus, had spiked wheels to help it travel along the moon's surface. It also had a cone-shaped collector to separate dust from rocks. One day, Lucia wants to become an engineer and work for NASA's Jet Propulsion Laboratory. She hopes to build rovers that will travel to Venus, Pluto, and Ceres.

Researchers test the Volatiles Investigating Polar Exploration Rover, or VIPER, mobile robot at NASA's Simulated Lunar Operations Lab in Ohio.

NASA hopes that their robot competitions will inspire young learners in STEM (science, technology, engineering, and math). They hope some of these students could be part of the next group of scientists working at their agency. But there are many more robot competitions through schools and other organizations for students to join.

The World Robot Olympiad (WRO) is a global robotic competition. Here children make a robot at the 2014 WRO.

Key Figure

Shriya Sawant is only fifteen years old but is already a well-known figure among student roboticists. For the 2022 Lunabotics Junior Contest, Shriya studied past NASA rovers. She planned seven different models and then built the winning robot for the older-grade competition. The RAD: Regolith Accretion Device had a bucket drum to dig up the moon's surface. The robot was made to work in low gravity and on rough surfaces.

Shriya Sawant looked to past NASA rovers for inspiration when she created the RAD: Regolith Accretion Device.

ROBOTS BUILT BY STUDENTS PLAY SOCCER IN 2014.

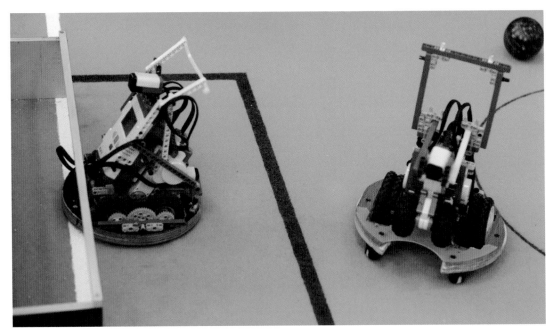

How Fun!

Competition robots are hardworking machines that can also be used for fun. Like all robots, they have a machine brain. This computer tells the robot what to do. Some competition robots are autonomous and act on their own while others are controlled by people. They also have sensors that help the machine feel, hear, and see. Batteries power these robots. And actuators such as wheels make it possible for competition robots to move.

Competition robots compete in events around the world. Students of all ages create robots and have fun with other kids that are interested in robotics. Some competitions, such as the Lunabotics Junior Contest, have students compete on their own. Other contests have teams of students compete against other teams. In some matches, teams design and program their robots to go the fastest or be the best at some special task.

Children compete at the 2014 WRO in Sochi, Russia.

Chapter 2

EARLY ROBOT COMPETITIONS

It's not entirely clear when robot competitions began, but a couple of events got them started.

In 1977, the Institute of Electrical and Electronics Engineers advertised an event for people to design small robots that would complete a maze. Almost six thousand people from around the world signed up.

The final event of the Amazing Micromouse Competition took place in June 1979. Fifteen tiny mouse machines competed. They had microcomputers and sensors that guided their actions through the maze. The robot Moonlight Express won by completing the maze the fastest at 30.04 seconds. Engineers from the state of Washington created it.

Within six years, Micromouse contests appeared in Europe and Japan. These competitions are still held around the world.

The final Amazing Micromouse Competition in June 1979

The creators of Moonlight Express, Ron Dilbeck, Art Boland, and Phil Stover (*second from left to right*), celebrate winning the 1979 Amazing Micromouse Competition.

Critter Crunch

The first Critter Crunch robot competition took place in 1989 in Denver, Colorado. At this event, robots battled one another. Members from the Denver Mad Scientists Club crafted the contest's rules. Robots had to weigh less than 20 pounds (9.1 kg) and be smaller than 12 x 12 x 12 inches (30.4 x 30.4 x 30.4 cm). Fewer than a dozen robots entered the competition. The robot Thing One was the winner.

STEM Spotlight

People that design and build robots write codes for them. Codes are written instructions that tell robots what to do. There are many kinds of coding. Some coding programs, such as Scratch and Python, use a drag-and-drop language. Other programs, such as Java, are also used for coding competition robots.

Chapter 3

MANY CHALLENGES

Each year, thousands of students go all out for robotics. Clubs design, build, program, and test their machines. They prepare for competitions.

For Inspiration and Recognition of Science and Technology (FIRST) is a robotics community. The group works to get young people excited about STEM by having them compete in robot competitions. In January 2022, tens of thousands of high school students attended the FIRST Robotics Competition Kickoff. At this event, FIRST announces the year's robotic challenge. Over three thousand teams from countries around the world geared up for the season. Every team tries their best to win. Competitors also have to show kindness and respect toward others.

Children in Libya compete at the 2022 FIRST Tech Challenge.

The FIRST Tech Challenge is one of many robot competitions for children around the world.

Teams celebrate winning the 2017 FIRST Robotics Regional Competition.

The 2022 FIRST World Championship ended with a tiebreaking match. Two teams, assigned the colors red and blue, each had three robots that could be up to about 4 feet (1.2 m) tall. The teams moved their robots around the game space to grab balls and shoot them into a basket to score a point. The high school team 1619 Up-A-Creek Robotics won the match. It was the first time a Colorado team won the FIRST World Championship.

Pitching In

The Robotics Education & Competition (REC) Foundation hosts a popular competition. Over a million students from seventy countries take part in REC's VEX robotic programs. They have programs for different age groups, which span from elementary school through college.

A game, called Pitching In, was the VEX IQ challenge in 2021 to 2022. During matches, students played alone or

Children of all ages participate in robotics programs globally.

In robotic competitions such as Pitching In, students can work alone or in teams. Here children compete during Robofest, a part of the 2018 WRO in Thailand.

in pairs and steered their robots to score points. Robots moved around the 6 x 8-foot (1.8 x 2.4 m) playing field. The teams could earn points in different ways, such as having their robots grab one of the balls and carry it to a special spot on the field. They could also shoot the ball into a square-shaped goal.

Underwater Robots

RoboSub is a competition for underwater robots. Autonomous underwater vehicles (AUVs) are planned, built, and tested by teams from around the world. In

2019, an all-woman team from Arizona State University (ASU) competed and took home third place. Team Desert WAVE, which stands for Women in Autonomous Vehicle Engineering, put their robot, Phoenix, through a series of tasks. It swam through gates and picked up objects in the 16-foot-deep (4.9 m) test pool. Sensors, including cameras and sonar, guided Phoenix.

There are many different robotic competitions every year. Engineers, teachers, parents, and business leaders know that these activities help students gain skills for the future.

In some robotic competitions, students design underwater robots such as the one shown here.

Key Figure

The members of Desert WAVE are all key figures and up-and-coming talent in robotics. Desert WAVE was formed in 2018 with the help of ASU and the Si Se Puede Foundation. Both groups encourage and support women in engineering. By competing in robot competitions, Desert WAVE members can build their engineering skills and gain knowledge that will benefit them in engineering and robotics careers.

ARIZONA STATE UNIVERSITY

Desert WAVE is an all-woman robotics team from ASU.

Chapter 4

FUTURE ROBOTICS

Soccer is not just a sport for people. In RoboCupJunior, robots compete in soccer games. There are two teams. Each team has two autonomous robots that play on a 52 x 76-inch (132 x 193 cm) carpeted playing field. Just like players in a soccer game, the robots have to get their ball into their opponent's goal to score. Each game lasts twenty minutes. The team with the most goals wins.

Chess grandmaster Garry Kasparov plays a game against the supercomputer Deep Blue in 1996.

A Grand Goal

In 1997, supercomputer Deep Blue beat the chess world champion. Scientists and engineers then wondered if computers could be used in other competitions. About three months later, the Robotics Cup, or RoboCup, soccer competitions began. Robotics experts hoped to mix the fun and excitement of soccer with the science of robots.

Deep Blue in 1996

RoboCup robots in 2019

They wanted to better understand artificial intelligence and improve technology. Now RoboCup has several kinds of contests, including one with humanoid soccer players.

The RoboCup league has one grand goal. By 2050, they plan to field a humanoid soccer team that can beat the most recent winner of the World Cup!

More to Come

Robotics and technology are the future. When FIRST robotics began in 1989, they started with only twenty-three teams. They wanted to create a new sport where any kid on their competition robot teams could become a pro. Fast-forward to 2022 and the VEX robotics programs are the largest in the world with over twenty thousand students competing in contests.

People watch a RoboCup soccer game in Australia in July 2019.

Children in Belarus build the Lego Mindstorms EV3 in 2019.

Being in a robotics club and joining competitions is exciting. Planning, building, and competing with your very own robot makes learning fun too. FIRST, RoboCup, VEX robotics, RoboSub, and all the other robotic competitions around the world bring students together. They know that science, technology, and robots are fun!

STUDENTS CAN START LEARNING ABOUT ROBOTICS AT ANY AGE.

Glossary

actuator: a tool for moving or controlling something

artificial intelligence: the ability of a computer or robot to think or perform tasks as intelligently as humans

autonomous: able to act on its own

engineer: a person who invents, designs, builds, and tests machines or other technology

humanoid: a robot with a human form or characteristics

microcomputer: a very small computer

model: a small copy of something that is used as a guide to make it in full size

roboticist: a person who builds and programs robots

robotics: technology dealing with robots

rover: a device that explores the surface of other extraterrestrial bodies

sensor: a device that finds and responds to something in an environment

supercomputer: a computer that performs at a high level

Learn More

Britannica Kids: Robot
    https://kids.britannica.com/students/article/robot/276749

Ceceri, Kathy. *Bots! Robotic Engineering: With Hands-On Makerspace Activities*. White River Junction, VT: Nomad, 2019.

Kenney, Karen Latchana. *Cutting-Edge Robotics*. Minneapolis: Lerner Publications, 2019.

Kulz, George Anthony. *Hobby and Competition Robots*. Minneapolis: Core Library, 2019.

National Geographic: What Is a Robot?
    https://education.nationalgeographic.org/resource/what-robot

PBS: "Me & My Robot"
    https://www.pbs.org/video/me-my-robot-scq2lo/

Index

autonomous, 8, 20–21, 23

Critter Crunch, 12

Desert WAVE, 21–22

engineers, 5, 10–11, 21–22, 24

For Inspiration and Recognition
of Science and Technology
(FIRST), 14, 18, 27–28

Grisanti, Lucia, 5

Lunabotics Junior Contest, 4–5, 7, 9

Micromouse contests, 10–11

Pitching In, 19

RoboCup, 24, 26, 28

Sawant, Shriya, 7

sensors, 8, 11, 21

Photo Acknowledgments

Image credits: NASA/Bridget Caswell, Alcyon Technical Services, p. 5; Martynova Anna/
shutterstock.com, pp. 6, 9; ASA/JPL-Caltech/MSSS, p. 7; Laura Lezza/Getty Images, p. 8; AP
Photo/Marty Lederhandler, pp. 10, 12; ABDULLAH DOMA/AFP via Getty Images, pp. 15, 16–17;
Andy Cross/The Denver Post via Getty Images, p. 18; Ground Picture/Shutterstock.com, p. 19;
tdee photo cm/Shutterstock.com, p. 20; Du Yang/China News Service via Getty Images, p. 21;
Thomas Trompeter/Shutterstock.com, p. 22; AP Photo/George Widman, p. 24; Yvonne Hemsey/
Getty Images, p. 25; PETER PARKS/AFP via Getty Images, p. 26; Xinhua/Bai Xuefei via Getty
Image, p. 27; AlesiaKan/Shutterstock.com, p. 28; Monkey Business Images/Shutterstock.com,
p. 29.

Cover: REUTERS/Mike Blake/Alamy Stock Photo.